Ladies First

Transformed Publishing

Mission: To Proclaim Transformation and Truth

Published by: Transformed Publishing
Website: www.transformedpublishing.com
Email: transfromedpublishing@gmail.com

ISBN: 978-1-953241-11-5
Printed in the U.S.A.

Ladies

First

Babette Bailey

Acknowledgements

First of all, I want to acknowledge all ladies and thank you for all the roles you have played from hair stylists to teachers, from designers to preachers, from receptionists to lawyers, from engineers to ballers, from cashiers to clerks, from doctors to nurses, from acquaintances to friends, from care takers to kin. I believe every lady plays a role in helping shape the lives of other ladies.

I want to show special appreciation to those who have been intentional in their efforts to pull others up, to help guide, to bless, to impart, to encourage, to invest, and to love.

Special thanks and acknowledgment to the ladies I call "ladies indeed" that took the time to share with me some very intimate and powerful details of their lives that they thought could give very strong insights for helping other ladies become "ladies indeed" - Pastor Sebrena Clark and Minister Barbette Williams. And to my publisher, Diana Robinson, for helping me turn this book into an amazing study; for her added insights, ideas, and guidance through every step; and for all she does that extends beyond the contract.

I want to acknowledge and thank my mother and wonderful sisters, who have played major roles in leading by example as quality ladies in how they have poured into every area of my life; my sisters-in-law; many of the other beautiful ladies at my church; and other wonderful ladies who I have met along my journey. Thank you.

To the awesome men who have played their roles in encouraging, supporting, and helping us to become beautiful and amazing ladies. To my dad, my Bishop, my brothers, brothers-in-law, my brothers in the Body of Christ, and many other awesome men of integrity and honor who have shown us how a real lady should be treated.

Most of all, I acknowledge God for His insights and His wonderful words of wisdom that are the ultimate guide to us becoming virtuous and amazing ladies; the kind of ladies men long to have and we long to be. I thank God for adorning us and for His amazing love that washes us, restores us, and waters us over and over again, till we become the beautiful flowers He has called us to be.

Table of Contents

1

Introduction

Introduction

Hello Ladies,

What comes to your mind when you hear the expression *ladies first*? Do you picture a man opening the door for a lady? Does an instant image flash in your mind of a man allowing a lady to order dinner first or speak first; or do you see a man simply allowing a lady to be first in everything?

Honestly, I was not thinking about any of that when the expression came to me. I was actually thinking about how we, as ladies, so many times focus on what men should do and who they should be, while we neglect striving to be the same.

I was thinking of some of the problems, we as women, have had in our relationships, and somehow, I ended up all the way back to Adam and Eve looking at how they both were casting blame, while both had played a part in the sin. I started realizing that we, as women, are just as responsible as the men for a great deal of the broken condition of our relationships. I concluded that if we can take the blame for eating the forbidden fruit first; meaning turning away from God and His righteousness, then we can also take the initiative first to get back in right standing with God. I reasoned that if we have the influence and the attitude to lead a man astray, maybe we can use that same influence and attitude to lead them back to the right way. But, we can't do it unless we get there first.

I personally have struggled with relationship after relationship, although I long to have a lasting, healthy, happy, and fulfilling relationship. Like many other women, I have read books, received counsel, prayed and fasted, and listened to teaching after teaching. I have tried withholding all, giving all, surrendering all, and every other thing suggested - it seems like I've tried it all. At 56 years old, I never imagined that I would still be single, still desiring and longing to have a wonderful, amazing, fulfilling, and blessed marriage.

At the same time, I have to admit that I have not done things the way I should, God's way. I've been unfaithful, impatient, doubtful, undisciplined, lustful, disobedient, rebellious, hypo-critical, backslidden, and all the things we accuse men of being. Though I've tried to do right, I've fallen time and time again. In all my failures, mistakes and struggles, I've come to understand that just as it is hard for women to do right, it is likewise hard for men and maybe even moreso because of the overall makeup and the mindset of the man verses the woman. And if we can't keep ourselves from doing wrong, falling short, making mistakes, and bad decisions, we can't expect men to either. I've found in trying to give God my all, my commitment, my wealth, my time, my trust, my heart, my best, my love, my first, my honesty, my submission, my sacrifice, etc.; that it is much like the man giving all these things to the woman. The same challenges we struggle with, making God our all, they struggle with - making us their all. Just like we miss it, they miss it and just like it's hard for us, and sometimes feels impossible, it's the same for the men. However, it is not impossible. Just like we can commit and devote our hearts and our lives to God and be sold out to loving God and doing the right things - so can a man do with us.

The vision and format for this book is to draw women together to reflect inwardly and express outwardly, and to create an atmosphere of encouragement and accountability. I feel that what God showed me is to stop blaming the man or looking to the man to do for me what I'm not doing for Him (God). In my effort to live for God and commit my life to God, I see the same challenges and issues the men deal with committing to us. Not only that, but I can see how we've often been guilty of doing the same things we've accused the men of doing; especially in this twenty first century. We've lusted, we've flirted, we've lied, we've walked out, we've cheated, we've been sneaky and dishonest, etc.

As I was talking and sharing my thoughts on *ladies first,* with some of our leading ladies (ladies indeed!), they began to share some heartfelt, enlightening, powerful, thought provoking, and encouraging insights that I thought were worth looking further into and sharing. So, included in this book are some of the experiences, the wisdom, and the understanding that I know will also have a profound effect on each reader desiring to develop a *ladies first* mindset.

Throughout this endeavor, I would like to hear your testimonies. Please email me directly at:

writeforyourevent@gmail.com

Sincerely,

Babette Bailey

What do you think of when you hear the words ladies first?

What things do you think we as ladies can look at doing first, that we often blame the men for not doing?

2

Insight

Insight

The insights in this book can and will impact our lives not only as ladies, but as wives, friends, mothers, sisters, leaders, partners, as females in general, and in every other relational position we hold. The focus is *ladies first*. What should we do first; ask first; try to understand first; apply first; change first; surrender first; etc.?

So many times, we feel like we've heard it all before; we've got it all together; we know what we're doing; we're equipped and ready; or like everybody is wrong, except us. We have even experienced times when we didn't want to hear another teaching, another preaching, another prophesy, or another video. We didn't want to read another book, another article, or another story. And we surely didn't want to talk about *it* anymore!

Let me encourage you as I encourage myself. Let's be the first to surrender, to listen, to try again, to invest, to stand, to live right, walk right, and talk right, to stop judging, to seek wisdom, to apply understanding, to love, and to go the extra mile in order to be the kind of ladies that we want and expect our men and others to be. Ladies – let's start by first taking a deeper look at ourselves and what it's going to take to develop the *ladies first* approach.

Describe a time when you lowered your expectations or gave up completely because you did not get the results you were looking for (when you wanted them).

What areas of your life require a greater level of discipline? Describe what those areas of your life would look like with a greater level of discipline.

3

Impactful

Impactful

Pastor Sebrena Clark, the wife of Bishop Merton L. Clark, the founder and senior pastor of Truth Revealed International Ministries of which I am a long-time member, asked me when I first got the idea or the theme of *Ladies First*. As I thought back, I remembered thinking and writing about this topic when I was working at the prison over 15 years ago. During this conversation, a sobering thought arose, *I had been struggling with this same issue over and over again all those years; kind of like the children of Israel going around the same mountain for 40 years, when the journey should have only taken 11 days.*

Deuteronomy 1:2-3
It is eleven days'
journey from
Horeb by way of
Mount Seir to
Kadesh Barnea. Now
it came to pass in the
fortieth year, in the
eleventh month, ...

Journal about a situation or a circumstance that you have tolerated too long.

I realized that my deliverance didn't have to take that long. Now I pray and strive to share with the hope that God can use what the enemy meant for evil, for good; and help prevent other women from wandering in the wilderness for as long as I have and deter some from going through the same struggles I have. I hope and pray that you will heed the warnings, accept the advice, follow the godly counsel, make the adjustments, and that you will experience the happy, healthy, and fulfilling relationships you long for and not continue to wander or remain *stuck* year after year.

The meal is prepared, ladies come and dine with us.

Genesis 50:20
But as for you, you meant evil against me;
but God meant it for good,
in order to bring it about as *it is* this day,
to save many people alive.

Ephesians 3:17-19
that Christ may dwell in your hearts through faith; that you,
being rooted and grounded in love, may be able to comprehend
with all the saints what *is* the width and length and depth and
height — to know the love of Christ which passes knowledge;
that you may be filled with all the fullness of God.

First Things First!

We've all heard that we must put God first. How important is it that we learn to put God first? Can we realistically put God first in everything? If so, how? One of the things the Bible tells us is that every good and perfect gift comes from God (*see* James 1:17). So looking for good and perfect lives and relationships apart from God, I believe is one of our biggest mistakes.

I have given much thought to the idea that we want our men to put us first, but how can a man who doesn't love God truly love us? How can they honor and respect us? And how can we truly love, honor, and respect them. In learning to love God and put God first, we learn how to love ourselves and others.

For a person to know God is to know love and to know *how* to love. To put God first, is to reverence God. When a person reverences God, they become mindful of what they do and think. This is all a matter of the heart. These things are true for men and women. We ladies want our men to be men of God, so we have to ensure we are women of God.

Use this space to reflect on the questions pondered above.

Continued...

4

Incapable

Incapable

We are incapable of genuine change without the transforming power of Jesus Christ!

Romans 15:13
Now may the God of hope fill you with all joy and peace in believing, that you may abound in hope by the power of the Holy Spirit.

Too many times, as ladies, we get stuck in bad relationships and bad situations. We say we want to change and are ready for change, but we keep walking away and going back. We act up and then give in; and just keep enduring because of our weaknesses. Minister Barbette says unfortunately, we'll stay in those same situations for years and it's not till we get sick and tired of our situation, will we change.

What does it mean to be *sick and tired of being sick and tired*? To me it means that situation and that bad relationship we've been enduring so long has us so physically and mentally overwhelmed, that we absolutely cannot tolerate it another day. Most of us have gone through so much more than we should have; hoping, praying, waiting, and wishing that our men would come to wholeheartedly love us in the way we desire to be loved. Many of us have endured abusive situations for years, all the while believing it was just temporary affliction - *every time would be the last time.*

We must admit many of us have at times neglected ourselves waiting for a man to come back to us or accept us. We have made excuses for their behavior. We have done all we can to measure up to their expectations and demands. We have even distanced ourselves from our family and friends.

We have run behind them. We have even accepted their mistreatment trying to maintain the relationship. We have taken them back time after time after they had been unfaithful or unreliable. Many times, we have been so tangled up that we couldn't even see the manipulation. We may have questioned whether we were the cause of their abuse, their leaving, the disrespect, and even the unfaithfulness to us.

Most of the time our friends and family see and know what is going on, even when they don't say anything. Their silence may be a result of them being sick and tired of trying to help someone who does not seem to want help or is just not ready to get out of the unfavorable situation. They want to help and they care but feel compelled to back off in order to keep the peace and preserve the relationship.

John 15:4-5
Abide in Me, and I in you. As the branch cannot bear fruit of itself, unless it abides in the vine, neither can you, unless you abide in Me. "I am the vine, you are the branches. He who abides in Me, and I in him, bears much fruit; for without Me you can do nothing.

Pastor Sebrena always reminds us we are not damsels in distress; helpless and waiting for somebody to rescue us. We have value! We are influential! We're intelligent! We shouldn't be looking for someone to take care of us, but to partner with us. With a healthy level of pride and balanced self-esteem we will not accept anyone looking down on us or talking down to us.

Hebrews 5:8
[T]hough He [Jesus] was a Son, *yet* He learned obedience by the things which He suffered.

Describe how you can relate to the thoughts expressed in this section.

Continued...

I know we all have come to realize that nothing is going to change until we change, and we are not going to change until we get sick and tired of the issues of longing, rejection, lies, shame, hurt, disrespect, doubt, confusion, fighting, and the list goes on and on.

Ladies we must get ourselves together! We're longing to be free! Once we are free, we can and will begin to get our strength back, our peace back, our minds back, and our lives back. Eventually, hope will arise again of finding real love. But first we must get past the trauma of what we have been through and be healed. Then we must get over the fear of getting tangled up in another bad relationship. So many of these things we realize and agree with, but still sometimes we need to be reminded of them or pushed toward them; and many times when we're caught up in these situations we can't think or see it for what *it* really is.

We must first be able to see ourselves realistically and recognize the things that are not good for us. We must believe and know God wants His best for us. God does not want us to take care of a man, endure abuse, neglect ourselves, or suffer needlessly thinking that is love. God wants us to know what love really is and He wants us to be loved.

I know I've been guilty of feeling like I've messed up so bad and disobeyed God to the point that I didn't think I deserved God's blessings. The truth is we have all fallen short of the glory of God and we all miss the mark. But God's love never fails, and nothing can separate us from His love. Are their consequences? Yes! There are natural laws, and even spiritual laws that play a part, but they don't stop God from loving us. And even if God chastens us, it's intended to help us get on the right track (*see* Hebrews 12:7-11).

Romans 8:35
Who shall separate us from the love of Christ? *Shall* tribulation, or distress, or persecution, or famine, or nakedness, or peril, or sword?

1 John 4:16
And we have known and believed the love that God has for us. God is love, and he who abides in love abides in God, and God in him.

Romans 3:22-24
[E]ven the righteousness of God, through faith in Jesus Christ, to all and on all who believe. For there is no difference; for all have sinned and fall short of the glory of God, being justified freely by His grace through the redemption that is in Christ Jesus [.]

Proverbs 10:22
The blessing of the Lord makes *one* rich, And He adds no sorrow with it.

Describe how you can relate to the thoughts expressed.

Incapable; without Christ.
Ladies, we have got to realize that
nothing is going to change, until we change.

Luke 18:27	*Romans 5:8*	*2 Timothy 2:13*
… "The things which are impossible with men are possible with God."	But God demonstrates His own love toward us, in that while we were still sinners, Christ died for us.	If we are faithless, He remains faithful; He cannot deny Himself.

Isaiah 55:8-9
"For My thoughts *are* not your thoughts, Nor *are* your ways My ways," says the Lord. "For *as* the heavens are higher than the earth, So are My ways higher than your ways, And My thoughts than your thoughts.["]

God's Word reminds us that even when we are unfaithful, God remains faithful. His love is unconditional, and His ways are not our ways nor His thoughts our thoughts. Like the Prodigal Son, even if we leave God, God is always ready with open arms for us to come back to Him (*see* Luke 15). He will clean us up and remind us that we are special; we have purpose and destiny; we are forgiven; and we are loved. God wants us to know that we have a Father in heaven who has freely given us the abundant *above all* blessing, confidence, and the authority to overcome every work of the enemy.

To see the power of the transforming glory of God in our lives, we must seek to know who God is and who God wants us to be. As we allow God to show us Himself and the truth about ourselves, we become transformed by the Word of God and His power; from the inside out. With this genuine transformation, our hopes and the desires we have longed for, begin being fulfilled.

Ephesians 1:3-7
Blessed *be* the God and Father of our Lord Jesus Christ, who has
blessed us with every spiritual blessing in the heavenly *places* in
Christ, just as He chose us in Him before the foundation of the
world, that we should be holy and without blame before Him in
love, having predestined us to adoption as sons by Jesus Christ to
Himself, according to the good pleasure of His will, to the praise
of the glory of His grace, by which He made us accepted in the
Beloved. In Him we have redemption through His blood, the
forgiveness of sins, according to the riches of His grace[.]

Reflect and write unto the Lord.

Psalm 139:13-18
For You formed my inward parts;
You covered me in my mother's womb.
I will praise You, for I am fearfully *and* wonderfully made;
Marvelous are Your works,
And *that* my soul knows very well.
My frame was not hidden from You,
When I was made in secret,
And skillfully wrought in the lowest parts of the earth.
Your eyes saw my substance, being yet unformed.
And in Your book they all were written,
The days fashioned for me,
When *as yet there were* none of them.
How precious also are Your thoughts to me, O God!
How great is the sum of them!
If I should count them,
they would be more in number than the sand;
When I awake, I am still with You.

Reflect and write unto the Lord.

5

Impartation

Impartation

Another awesome point that Minster Barbette makes is that:
It is vital that we first learn to be ladies.

How do we learn to be ladies?

One of the main ways we learn to be ladies is by sitting under the counsel and teaching of other ladies. Specifically, ladies who love God; who know how to carry themselves; who value themselves and others; and ladies who are willing and able to help develop other ladies. Ladies who have gone through the process of learning who they are and whose they are can then impart in us valuable insights that will help shape us as well.

We must truly look within and get to know ourselves in order for the work that needs to be done to take place. Ask yourself, *how do you feel about yourself?* It is imperative for us to stop blaming everyone else for where we are and where we are not and take accountability for the choices we've made. Every time I want to blame a man for mistreating me or for any of the problems I may have gone through, I'm constantly reminded that I was the one who stayed and allowed it and I must take responsibility for my share of the blame.

Now as we prepare ourselves for our kings by becoming what we want to attract, Pastor Sebrena encourages us that the best place to start is by forgiving ourselves and others. I think that's an excellent idea, and a great way to wipe the slate clean and start over. We cannot be forgiven if we don't forgive (*see* Mathew 6:15), and many of us need to stop beating ourselves up and start loving and encouraging ourselves.

26

Describe characteristics of ladies you have known or observed that you would like to emulate.

How do you feel about yourself?

Identify a person, personal choice, or life area where you are harboring unforgiveness. Will you make a quality decision to forgive? What steps must you take?

No one likes constructive criticism or to be told they are wrong, but we all have areas where we need to grow, where we need to change, that can hinder our productivity, and where we could use Godly counsel. The following are just a few areas that I want to expound on:

- ❖ Self-Esteem
- ❖ Physical Fitness
- ❖ Adultery
- ❖ Same-Sex Attractions
- ❖ Cleanliness
- ❖ Education
- ❖ Aggressive & Loud Behaviors
- ❖ Appearances
- ❖ Self Control / Discipline

As we touch on these subjects just briefly, take a look inside and ask yourself where you are and if you could use some Godly counsel. Some of these things we've heard before, yet we continue to struggle because we haven't fully understood how devastating they can be.

What can ladies do first to overcome low self-esteem and insecurity and begin to have a healthy and balanced view of themselves - not overly confident nor under confident?

One way to develop our self-confidence and overcome insecurity is by having a certain level of pride in ourselves. We need to love ourselves enough to avoid the wolves in sheep's clothing or the "dogs" that will sniff out and prey on those who are weak, fearful, and easily manipulated. We must learn how to speak up for ourselves as well and have standards that we refuse to compromise. We must do the things and achieve the goals that help us feel good about ourselves, instead of waiting for others to affirm us, or dictate to us what we're worth. We must be the first to tell ourselves we're valuable.

2 Timothy 3:6-7
For of this sort are those who creep into households and make captives of gullible women loaded down with sins, led away by various lusts, always learning and never able to come to the knowledge of the truth.

What about same-sex attractions?

I wanted to touch on this topic because I'm seeing more and more ladies led astray by this evil spirit. I am also very sensitive to this issue because it has affected someone who I love and care for very much. I don't discuss it lightly. I feel it definitely needs to be addressed. I think it's much like any fleshly addiction or stronghold. Once something brings satisfaction to our flesh, the door is opened for it to consume our flesh. After this threshold is passed, we can't see it for what it really is without the Spirit of God convicting us. We can't get free of it without the power of God delivering us. Like fornication, pornography, infidelity, and every other form of sexual immorality, it is wrong. It is against the will of God and sin against the body.

As a child, I had an unfortunate encounter with this spirit, but by the grace of God and His Spirit within me, that is not a struggle or a temptation for me.

I am sharing with the hope that those who are affected can take a serious look at this and seriously consider that it is wrong and why; and they can know that many have been delivered and that God can deliver them as well.

The Bible says in 1 Corinthians 7:9, "but if they cannot exercise self-control, let them marry. For it is better to marry than to burn *with passion.*" This scripture lets me know that sexual desires can be so great that they are hard to control. Through conversations I have had with women who have been in same-sex relationships, I found out that some women with same-sex attractions prey upon ladies just like men do, specifically, ladies who have been abused by men, and/or ladies who don't know God, the Truth of His Word, nor who they are in Christ.

God's Word says it is not His will for a man to lie down with another man as he would with a woman and those who practice homosexuality, and other forms of sexual immorality, will not inherit the Kingdom of God (*see* Romans 1:18-32 and 1 Corinthians 6:9-11).

Nobody wants to feel judged or condemned and I am not sharing a message of judgement or condemnation. My hope is that all will know God, and love and obey God, so they may have eternal life in heaven. To me, that's not judgement; it is compassion and love. Please hear my heart, and the hearts of those who are reaching out to you.

God's Design

1 Corinthians 6:18
Flee sexual immorality. Every sin that a man does is outside the body, but he who commits sexual immorality sins against his own body.

Genesis 2:18
And the Lord God said, "*It* is not good that man should be alone; I will make him a helper comparable to him."

Genesis 2:24
Therefore a man shall leave his father and mother and be joined to his wife, and they shall become one flesh.

Matthew 19:4-6
And He [Jesus] answered and said to them, "Have you not read that He who made *them* at the beginning 'made them male and female,' and said, 'For this reason a man shall leave his father and mother and be joined to his wife, and the two shall become one flesh'? So then, they are no longer two but one flesh. Therefore what God has joined together, let not man separate."

Ephesians 5:22-33
Wives, submit to your own husbands, as to the Lord. For the husband is head of the wife, as also Christ is head of the church; and He is the Savior of the body. Therefore, just as the church is subject to Christ, so *let* the wives *be* to

their own husbands in everything. Husbands, love your wives,
just as Christ also loved the church and gave Himself for her,
that He might sanctify and cleanse her with the washing of
water by the word, that He might present her to Himself a
glorious church, not having spot or wrinkle or any such thing,
but that she should be holy and without blemish. So husbands
ought to love their own wives as their own bodies; he who loves
his wife loves himself. For no one ever hated his own flesh, but
nourishes and cherishes it, just as the Lord *does* the church
For we are members of His body, of His flesh and of His bones.
"For this reason a man shall leave his father and mother and be
joined to his wife, and the two shall become one flesh."
This is a great mystery, but I speak concerning Christ
and the church. Nevertheless let each one of you
in particular so love his own wife as himself,
and let the wife *see* that she respects *her* husband.

Reflection:

❖ *It was the Lord that said He was making Adam a helper
comparable to him; not the same as Adam. Comparable
means of equivalent quality; worthy of comparison.*

❖ *God uniquely designed the male and female
body with attributes to become one flesh.*

❖ *Jesus reemphasized, "…they are no longer two
but one flesh. Therefore what God has
joined together, let not man separate."*

❖ *Paul expounded on this revelation, comparing the marriage
union between a man and a woman, to Christ and the
church. This illuminates the holiness of God's Design
for marriage between a man and a woman.*

Use this journal space to reflect on God's Design for marriage.

How do ladies get themselves together first physically?

Sometimes it's hard, but it's another area where we must learn to love ourselves. We may have to get help, but we need to get moving. Many ladies do not even like themselves and are not happy with where they are in life, but they want others to accept them. We don't have to be a size 7 or kill ourselves trying to measure up to someone else's standards, but we know when we need to work on ourselves, love ourselves more, and be honest with ourselves.

I believe this is one of our main struggles, so I don't want to run past this. At the same time, we've been battling with it so much I don't want to drill it anymore neither. I only want to encourage you to keep striving and not to give up.

Why do ladies become the other woman and how do they get out of those situations?

1 Corinthians 10:12 Therefore let him who thinks he stands take heed lest he fall.

It can happen and it does happen. Many times, we don't see it coming and we don't think it can happen to us, until it happens. I know I'm not the only one who has found myself in that situation before. When I went through it, the man I became involved with lied and I didn't know about the other lady. By the time I found out, my heart and flesh were already entangled. Once your flesh and heart get wrapped up, it's very hard and very painful to get untangled; but wanting to live right, determining to live right, and knowing what's right are mandatory in order for us to begin to get ourselves free.

Being disciplined and self-controlled also play major roles in avoiding getting tangled up and getting free if we do get tangled up. We cannot let our emotions or our flesh override what's right and self-love! Practicing these traits when we meet potential mates and when we're dating will allow us time to objectively build and grow the kind of relationships we want and that God desires for us.

In addition, both as single and married ladies, we need to be aware of our interactions with men, whether they are married or single themselves. We should consider how the other ladies feel that may be involved, how God feels about our interactions, and how our actions may look or be portrayed overall.

It is never too early to begin to honor your future spouse, even if you have not met them yet. We can avoid dishonoring others' marriages by maintaining a *ladies first* approach when interacting with all men. We can begin carrying ourselves as if we're already married. Avoid flirting. Avoid coarse joking. Avoid any kind of interacting that you would not do as a married woman.

Participate in this conversation by choosing a topic for personal reflection: self-esteem, physical fitness, or adultery.

How important is cleanliness to you?

Cleanliness indeed speaks to our character, as well as our level of maturity. I believe it does indeed make a difference in the kind of men we attract or run away. We need to not only clean up our act, but our kitchens, our bathrooms, our bodies, our mouths, our hair, our children, our laundry rooms, our cars, etc.

They say cleanliness is next to godliness. This may not be Biblical, but if you think about it, it has a lot of truth to it. Think about the people you know who are not clean and those who are.

1 Corinthians 6:19-20
Or do you not know that your body is the temple of the Holy Spirit *who is* in you, whom you have from God, and you are not your own? For you were bought at a price; therefore glorify God in your body and in your spirit, which are God's.

Reflect and write unto the Lord.

Is education really important? Why or why not?

Once again, I think it's unfair for us to expect the man to be all that we're not willing to be. Whatever we do for ourselves speaks to how we feel about ourselves, and our level of character and integrity. Our actions speak and, in some ways, tell people how they can treat us. Having a better education helps to open doors for better jobs and opportunities for us. It also helps us feel better about ourselves. It is not only about having degrees and certifications. Education is an opportunity to become more knowledgeable about different things in life like plants, children, art, music, God's Word, etc. It also gives us the opportunity to create better incomes and better incomes open better doors. Being educated or knowledgeable better equips us to come alongside our men and support them by the wisdom, knowledge, and intellect, etc., that we can offer about different things, such as, budgeting and finances, children and families, health and wellness, laws and regulations, etc.

Being educated or knowledgeable about the Word of God helps us in many ways. It makes us hopeful; it increases our faith; we are able to stand on the promises of God; we know the commands and expectations of God for us; and we are better equipped to walk in the will of God for our lives. Any kind of knowledge gives us a sense of purpose and a greater ability to communicate and even teach others. What if we were more knowledgeable about how to have successful relationships and how to love and be loved? We may not be able to get back what we've forfeited because of our ignorance in the past, but we don't have to continue in that ignorance.

Proverbs 1:5, 7
A wise *man* will hear and increase learning,
And a man of understanding will attain wise counsel,
The fear of the Lord *is* the beginning of knowledge,
But fools despise wisdom and instruction.

Reflect and write unto the Lord.

Psalm 111:10
The fear of the Lord *is*
the beginning of
wisdom; A good
understanding have
all those who do
His commandments.
His praise
endures forever.

Should ladies have aggressive and loud personalities?

I do agree that some ladies are naturally loud and some of it comes from our upbringing, but there is such a thing as too loud and too aggressive. We are all born in sin and shaped in iniquity, and we all have areas in our lives where we need to learn to be more disciplined and self-controlled. Many can say, *this is who I am and I'm not going to change!* But who can say to God, *this is just who I am?* Even when we say it to people, it is wrong; especially when we're connected or seeking to be connected to God. In order to get along, we all must bend, and stretch, and wait, and share, etc. We want others to bend (mainly our men - so we too must endeavor to make adjustments).

As ladies, we are encouraged to be quiet and submissive. This doesn't mean we can't have a voice; just that we don't have to yell and be combative or aggressive to get our point across. One scripture says we can win our unbelieving husbands over with the way we live; that includes the way we speak. Another scripture says we are to adorn ourselves with modesty and self-control. Truth be told, some of that aggression comes from a lack of control and a lack of wisdom and even submission. Sometimes, how we act can have a very negative impact on our relationships, our families, our jobs, our friendships, etc. We must take a deeper look and see if we are being aggressive, negative, pessimistic, mean, angry, combative, stubborn, jealous, vengeful, etc. All these things can affect how we act and interact with people. I have battled with all these things, and I'm mindful that I must continue to grow and always check myself in these areas.

One thing Pastor Sebrena really helped me to see in myself and understand that could be a major factor in some of my aggression, is that as a single parent for so many years, I've had to play the role of a father as well as a mother, and that's one of the things I will need to be aware of and strive to be balanced in.

1 Peter 3:1-7

Wives, likewise, *be* submissive to your own husbands, that
even if some do not obey the word, they, without a word,
may be won by the conduct of their wives, when they observe
your chaste conduct *accompanied* by fear. Do not let your
adornment be *merely* outward - arranging the hair, wearing
gold, or putting on *fine* apparel - rather *let it be* the hidden
person of the heart, with the incorruptible *beauty* of a gentle
and quiet spirit, which is very precious in the sight of God.
For in this manner, in former times, the holy women who
trusted in God also adorned themselves, being submissive to
their own husbands, as Sarah obeyed Abraham, calling him
lord, whose daughters you are if you do good and are not
afraid with any terror. Husbands, likewise, dwell with *them*
with understanding, giving honor to the wife, as to the
weaker vessel, and as *being* heirs together of the
grace of life, that your prayers may not be hindered.

What does this mean to you?

I've often heard that one of the most important things is that men need to be respected. We can tear them down with our words or build them up. In that, I know it is very important for us to learn to build men up and not tear them down.

I have found myself on many occasions yelling and arguing back and forth with a man. I've seen other women yelling and cursing at their men, embarrassing them and belittling them; trying to control and manipulate. I've learned that it comes moreso from pain and frustration than it does from actually being angry, and that we need to identify what we're really feeling. I do believe we should voice our concerns and even our opinions, but I don't believe it should be with yelling, and definitely not with cursing. Ladies, if a man can be too loud, surely a lady can too. And if he should not yell and curse, it's definitely not lady-like for us to do so. This will require us making the effort and being intentional, but we can change.

What do you think are the causes for loud and aggressive personalities - as well as for yelling and arguing? Do you think it is wrong? Why or why not?

Should appearance matter and does it matter?
How can we make ourselves more attractive?

Pastor Sebrena says, of course appearance matters, but she believes men like different things and that change and occasional surprises are good. To some, dressing in jeans and a t-shirt is sexy. Some think make-up and fancy hairdos are attractive. I think we can all definitely agree that some do not care about those things at all. They are moved by our personalities and character, by ladies who are fun and adventurous, or playful and laid back.

The best thing to do, is to be ourselves. Trying to measure up to the expectations another person can put on us can be discouraging, frustrating, and impossible. Having to go to bed with makeup on and having to be made up every day can be overwhelming. No one wants to be a slave to performance. At the same time, there is nothing wrong with trying to be presentable or looking nice especially on special occasions.

The last four topics we addressed are very practical:
cleanliness, education, aggressive and loud personalities, and
appearances. Use this journal space to reflect on at least one of
these topics. Outline action steps to make positive changes.

Continued...

6

Inclined to Marry?
An Honest Perspective

Inclined to Marry?
An Honest Perspective

Let's take an honest look at
the role of a wife or a potential wife.

I haven't heard too many ladies say they didn't want to be married. Even some of the ones that did claim they didn't want to be married, ended up marrying. Why? I think it's because inside all of us is that desire to be in love or have that special someone in our life, even though sometimes it gets buried and locked away – sometimes because of the traumas and heartbreaks we've seen and experienced. It may even appear to be dead until the right person comes along. To those who may feel like they are just too old to marry, or even think about it anymore, my mother remarried at the age of eighty-four, fulfilling the desire she still had within her.

Some of the issues we need to consider are how can we know if we are truly equipped and ready to marry? How much thought have we given to marriage besides our fleshly desires? Why are so many marriages struggling and failing? What about when there are disagreements, issues with finances, unfulfilled needs and expectations, opposing opinions regarding one another's friends or family members, and other things that can seriously challenge our relationships? What about 'for better or worse...'? What about counsel and effective communication? What do you feel is the wife's role or the husband's role? Preparation is vital to having and maintaining a happy and successful marriage. We also need wisdom and understanding, lest we keep making the same mistakes and keep struggling and suffering needlessly.

I was doing some introspection and thinking about some of the issues I've had with men. I realize that men can be very sensitive and need to feel loved and needed just like ladies do. It is written in the Word of God that we can win over our men, even the unbelieving man with submission, purity, reverence, and a gentle and quiet spirit. Many times, what we're seeing in the man is a reflection of ourselves; meaning when they feel they are being loved, appreciated, nurtured and built up, that's what will come out of them.

It is vital that we learn to see the good and stop focusing on all that we feel is not good.

It's sometimes easier to focus on all that the man is *not* doing instead of highlighting all that he is doing. This may require more practice for some, while for others it may come naturally, but it's necessary. Some women really know how to praise their man and build him up. We can practice by praising and exalting God for all He has done and all that He's doing. Let's decide in our hearts that there's no more tearing down. Let's help them where they need our help; even when they don't know it (lol). And while we can't afford to compromise our values and principles, we still must make room for growth, misunderstandings, and forgiveness.

An Open Perspective:
Sex is also one of the major areas we must examine and consider (i.e. before marriage; in the marriage; when the babies come; after the kids leave home; when there's been molestation or rape; and/or lust and perversion).

I know ladies who are almost worse than men, who are like nymphomaniacs, and who can't keep their clothes on. I know others who don't want a man to touch them, not even their own. But I've never known a man who didn't want some form of fulfillment.

I remember looking at a man one day in a lustful way (just keeping it real) and thinking to myself, like they say, WWJD – *What Would Jesus Do*? I was thinking, what would Pastor Sebrena or

Minister Barbette do? To me a classy lady or especially a woman of God would not be lusting after a man. Realistically it's one of those areas that many ladies need to grow in.

Sex before marriage - God's Word says it's against the will of God. Therefore, to be in right standing, we must wait for marriage. While we're waiting, we need to pay attention to what's going on with who we are dating. We don't want a pervert. We don't want someone we can't trust to be faithful. And we don't want someone who doesn't respect our feelings and opinions. So we must endeavor to be patient, self-controlled, intentional, and wise. We must be the ladies we want to be treated like.

One of the first things Pastor Sebrena reflected on was her first marriage. She wished she had listened to her father. He told her she was working too hard and doing too much; and that the man needed to chase after her and come to her. Her brothers were trying to protect her as well. God was speaking through them, but she couldn't see it. She and her mother were making excuses for his behavior because of his money and their emotions. She ended up having to leave everything she owned with only the clothes on her back to get away from him. Her dad wired her money to get back home. One lesson she learned is that "...in the multitude of counselors *there* is safety" (Proverbs 11:14).

Sometimes we as women, pursue men, even when they don't want us, but it should be the other way around. They should be 'blowing' our phone up, and 'chasing' us. Minister Barbette shared that when we chase a man, we will always have to chase him. She talked about how her husband, "Michael B.", she calls him, told her the first day they met that he was going to be her husband. Her response was, no he wasn't. He continued to tell her that she wasn't ready yet, but when she was ready, he would be right there. She said, for the next two years, he didn't push, but he made his presence known and was always in close proximity. He saw her at her worst, but he told her that none of that stuff moved him because she was his wife. Two years after they met, they were married, and have been together for twenty-seven plus years. This is not a fairy tale. This is real, and their love for each other speaks louder than words. She encourages ladies to know that we add value; even in our imperfection, we are valuable. Yes, we should strive to be cleansed, as demonstrated in Psalm 51, which speaks of getting rid of the impurities. All that stuff has to come out. But still, even where we are, we must know that we have value.

Another awesome perspective Pastor Sebrena shared is on the "Investor's Dream". She says if he is an investor, he's going to have something to invest! In order for him to invest in us he must see something worth investing in. We need to be whole and balanced; spirit, soul, and body. We need to be whole, because if we enter into the right relationship tainted and traumatized from past hurts and destructive relationships, we can end up taking it out on a good man and holding him hostage for what someone else has done. We need to know God and know the truth. If we're not led by the Spirit of God, we will be trying to change everything about ourselves to be accepted. One of Pastor Sebrena's favorite scriptures is Ephesians 1:6, "...He made us accepted in the Beloved." We should not have to lose weight, endure any kind of abuse, or be a fan in the stands (always cheering him on). We are to give our whole selves to God and take care of our bodies as temples of God. Endeavoring to follow him, as He follows God.

Proverbs 18:22
He who finds a wife finds a good *thing,* And obtains favor from the Lord.

As I think of some of the other personal struggles I've had in my relationships and my quest for love and marriage, I think of being double-minded. The Bible says a double-minded man is unstable in all his ways (*see* James 1:8). That's exactly how I have felt - unstable. I've been lustful, jealous, uncontrolled, unforgiving, controlling, insecure, stubborn, selfish, self-centered, disrespect-ful, inconsiderate, basically all that I've accused the men of being. I know how easy it is to be the one wrong and not even realize it.

Trying to get myself together has given me a whole different perspective on what men go through when they are trying to change their bad habits and old ways. Trying to let go of the man I felt like I was so in love with has been extremely hard, but I knew in order for me to get what I want, I had to let go of what I had. I had been compromising my beliefs, my needs, my heart, my friendships, and my God. I had waited, prayed, even pleaded with him about the right thing to do; which I felt was to marry. He didn't feel we should marry but was okay continuing our relationship as it was. Staying in that caused me to be in today and out every time I got hurt by all the wrong things I compromised on and the painful consequences of doing wrong. It was hard because in a way it felt like I was going from having something to having nothing. But the truth is I'm moving toward having what I truly desire and long for, and away from temporary gratification and a part time fix. I'm definitely not losing according to God's scale.

When it comes to marriage, two incomplete people do not make one another whole. Marriage is designed for two whole people to come together and complement one another. God has a plan for people as individuals and He also has a plan for the marriage union. Use this space to reflect on your views about where you are now and where you want to be in marriage.

Continued...

7

Influential
Leading Ladies of the Bible

Influential
Leading Ladies of the Bible

Exploring key attributes of some of the leading ladies of the Bible that can help us become the leading ladies of today:

Abigail

1 Samuel 25

The Bible says she was married to Nabal. (A man whose name means *foolish*.) She was his wife; whether by an arranged marriage or choice, and the law was that wives are to submit to their husbands. But Abigail had to make a decision for herself and those she cared for that would affect their lives, just as we will.

It is always good and right to follow God and the leading of His Holy Spirit. When her husband refused to provide food and drink for King David and his army, Abigail ran after the king and apologized for her husband's behavior and provided for him and his men; sparing the lives that the king was about to destroy in his rage.

Nabal, Abigail's husband, died *after* about ten days and Abigail ended up marrying King David.

Read 1 Samuel 25 and reflect.
What are your feelings about how Abigail handled herself when she went against her husband's decision?

Continued...

Hannah

1 Samuel 1 & 2

Elkanah had two wives, Hannah and Peninnah. Hannah longed to have a child, but year after year she could not conceive while Peninnah continued to have children and taunt Hannah because she could not. Even though Elkanah loved Hannah and would do anything he could for her, he could not make her able to conceive.

Hannah knew that God was the only one who could turn her situation around. She didn't go to anyone else. She stayed before God in prayer, pouring her heart and soul out to Him. She vowed to bless God in return for His blessing to her, and she was rewarded. She endured for years before she received what she had been praying for, but she didn't give up.

She touched the heart of God in a special way. I believe that if we as ladies can learn to touch the heart of God, it will not only affect our lives, but the lives of our children, our families, and others.

I was thinking of some of the people that cried out to God and touched His heart. They were healed, set free, changed, strengthened, protected, forgiven, restored, victorious, etc. I encourage you in the things you're longing and praying for - don't stop praying and pouring your heart out to God.

Read 1 Samuel chapters 1 & 2 and reflect.
Write about an impossible situation in your life that
you know only God can and will turn around.

Continued...

Gomer
Hosea 1

Gomer, the wife of Hosea the priest, kept going outside of her marriage and sleeping with other men; even having children with other men. But the Bible tells us that Hosea was told to take her as his wife; an illustration of God's love for His people who were constantly unfaithful to Him, yet still He loved them. He even sent Hosea out to recover Gomer after she would have been considered 'used up' and worthless. This speaks of how great God's love for us is, in spite of us. It's amazing and nothing can compare with His love. Nothing is as powerful and strong as His love. If God can love this woman to this extent and send someone in her life that will love her in spite of what she's done, how much more can God do it for us. Don't let anyone tell you you're not worthy of love.

Read Hosea 1 and the scriptures recorded here.

Jeremiah 3:14 "Return, O backsliding children," says the Lord; "for I am married to you. I will take you, one from a city and two from a family, and I will bring you to Zion.["]

1 Peter 4:8 And above all things have fervent love for one another, for "love will cover a multitude of sins."

Luke 7:47 ["]Therefore I say to you, her sins, which are many, are forgiven, for she loved much. But to whom little is forgiven, the same loves little."

Reflect on the love of God as you write unto the Lord.

Continued...

Tamar

2 Samuel 13

Tamar, the sister of Absalom, was raped by her half-brother and then abandoned. Many women have been traumatized through sexual experiences; even acts by those who claimed to love them. Some ladies have been left in a fallen state, never having recovered from the shame or the confusion and hurt. How is it possible for these ladies to recover?

Many could feel as broken, lost, and hopeless as Tamar; if not for the mercy, the love, the power, the grace, and the goodness of God. The Lord is healing, restoring, turning lives around, and using what the enemy meant for evil to bless others with their transparency, testimonies, help, and their willingness and boldness to fight for themselves and others.

Be encouraged and know that you can rise above the shame, the abuse, the hurt, and the trauma by the amazing love of God.

Read 2 Samuel 13 and the scriptures recorded here.

Psalm 147:3 He heals the brokenhearted
And binds up their wounds.

1 Peter 5:7 casting all your care upon Him,
for He cares for you.

Isaiah 61:1-3 "The Spirit of the Lord God is upon Me,
Because the Lord has anointed Me
To preach good tidings to the poor;
He has sent Me to heal the brokenhearted,
To proclaim liberty to the captives,
And the opening of the prison to those who are bound;
To proclaim the acceptable year of the Lord,
And the day of vengeance of our God;
To comfort all who mourn,
To console those who mourn in Zion,
To give them beauty for ashes,
The oil of joy for mourning,
The garment of praise for the spirit of heaviness;
That they may be called trees of righteousness,
The planting of the Lord, that He may be glorified."

Release the ashes and allow Jesus to heal broken heartedness and bind up wounds as you write unto the Lord.

Ruth

The Book of Ruth

Ruth was the daughter-in-law of Naomi. Ruth also had another daughter-in-law, Orpah, who was married to her other son. When Naomi lost her husband and both her sons, she told her two daughters-in-law to go back to their families while she was returning to her homeland. Ruth refused to depart from Naomi and vowed to stay with her, to follow her, and even make Naomi's God her God.

To me, Ruth surrendered all. She wasn't asking for anything, looking for anything, expecting anything, or trying to bargain. She only wanted to give. She had a faith and a resolve on the inside that most of us want, but struggle to achieve because we're holding on to too much; the past, broken or abandoned dreams, bitterness, selfishness, pain, etc. Ruth followed the counsel of Naomi without question and without being worried about possible repercussions.

Our famous Ruth: Why did she follow Naomi? Why did she respond differently than her sister-in law Orpah? What did it mean when she went to lay at Boaz's feet?

Read the book of Ruth and reflect
on the questions stated above.

Continued...

Bathsheba

2 Samuel 11

Bathsheba was the beautiful lady that King David saw bathing. He sent for her to have sex with him while her husband was away at war. She ended up pregnant from David. David tried to cover it up by sending for her husband so he could sleep with her, but he refused to sleep with her while the rest of the men were at war. So, then David had him put on the front lines in the battle and he was killed. David married Bathsheba, but the baby died.

Could Bathsheba have done anything to prevent what happened with David the king? Was she supposed to just remain quiet and go along with everything that happened? What about ladies today? We are the weaker vessels, but we still have a voice. We can still make an effort to do the right thing. Some say that's a tough situation! To first of all, be wanted by the king; then to go against the king! But I heard someone else say they don't think she was as innocent as we make her out to be.

I believe, in life, there are some things that will be very confusing and way too big for us to comprehend. We desperately need God. If we don't know God, and if we're not prayed up, and walking in the Spirit, it's going to cost us.

Read 2 Samuel 11 and the scriptures recorded here.

1 Peter 3:7 Husbands, likewise, dwell with them with understanding, giving honor to the wife, as to the weaker vessel, and as being heirs together of the grace of life, that your prayers may not be hindered.

1 Peter 5:8 Be sober, be vigilant; because your adversary the devil walks about like a roaring lion, seeking whom he may devour.

1 John 4:1 Beloved, do not believe every spirit,
but test the spirits, whether they are of God;
because many false prophets have gone out into the world.

The bible continuously calls us to honor authority
and to test the spirits to avoid becoming entangled in snares.
This is a lot to balance, therefore, we must
be tuned into the Voice of God for direction.

Take some time to listen and reflect on upcoming
decisions you have to make in this journal space.

Continued...

Queen Vashti & Queen Esther

The Book of Esther

Queen Vashti was married to the king, but when requested by the king to come to his banquet she refused as she was having her own banquet. Because it was done publicly, the king was encouraged to deal shrewdly with her so her disrespect would not be an encouragement for other women to do the same to their husbands.

Queen Esther ended up being Queen Vashti's replacement. She too was confronted with the decision to go before the king unsummoned and risk disrespecting protocol. Because her life and the life of the Jews were on the line, she had to take that risk. But before she did, she sought the Lord with fasting and prayer - even calling on the Jews to fast and pray with her. Her life was spared, and she preserved the lives of her people.

What do you think was the major difference between these ladies? Do you think Queen Vashti was wronged? How should we look at people who are divorced and those who remarry? It happens and it's hurtful; but is it possible that we have been a part of the cause? And how do we pick up the pieces and move on when all hope is lost?

I believe some of the things we endure are because of our own mistakes and bad decisions. Some of what we go through is because of outside influence. And sometimes we may just be caught up in a bad situation.

On the other hand, we may be the one to benefit from someone else's mistakes or misfortune. And like Esther we may be the one who comes along when his heart is wounded and after he has learned the valuable lessons that make the difference in loving and saving those he loves. If we are wise, if we are ready, if we are in position, if we are the one chosen - we can win the heart and maintain the heart of a king.

*Read the book of Esther and
reflect on the questions stated.*

Continued...

Mary, the mother of Jesus

Matthew 1:18-25; Luke 1:26-38

Mary was chosen by God to carry baby Jesus, and to be His mother. Though she was a virgin, she believed this miracle could be done. There were risks involved and her integrity and life would be on the line, but she chose to serve and believe God in the face of adversity.

Mary, to me, represents true humility, purity, and that childlike faith. She submitted completely to the purposes and the plan of God for her life. Like Mary, I know God sees and knows what's inside of us. He may choose someone that doesn't even know what they have in themselves.

What about the famous Mary, the mother of Jesus? I'm sure many women feel that they would love to be used of God in such an amazing way. Why Mary? Do you believe that God has planted something wonderful on the inside of all women that can be birthed into something amazing, *if* we would trust and submit to the plan of God, no matter how farfetched, how dangerous, or how impossible it may seem?

Read the scriptures noted and
reflect on the questions stated above.

Continued...

Rachel & Leah

This story begins in Genesis 29.

Rachel and Leah were not only two women dealing with the same man, they were two sisters. One Jacob loved and one was manipulated into the situation. Jacob loved Rachel and she was the one he chose, but Leah was given to Jacob by her father on the wedding night instead of Rachel. After working for Rachel for seven years, he ended up working another seven years and being married to them both. Leah was having the babies, but Rachel was barren. Both ladies were saddened by their situations; Rachel because she longed to give Jacob a child and Leah because no matter how many children she had; she did not feel loved. Whose fault was all of this? Can we tie it to anything happening in our world today? What things can we learn from these ladies?

Like their incredibly bizarre story, there are some crazy, ugly, mind blowing, and unbelievable things happening today, just like there were then. We don't know how we have gotten to some of the places we have found ourselves in, but I like what Leah did. She finally came to that place of giving God all the praise. It didn't matter anymore what it looked like, she found out the main thing was her relationship with God. She saw how in spite of all she was going through and had been through, God had truly blessed her and been with her, and she gave Him praise.

In my opinion, they both were innocent. Rachel suffered as much as Leah, though her struggle and her suffering wasn't the same. She may have had to learn some humility by the things she suffered. Can you imagine her always feeling like she was better than Leah because she was the pretty one? Have you ever had to be delivered from pride because of your body or your looks? Have you ever had to come to the realization that looks aren't everything? We all need the grace, the mercy, the goodness, the power, the love, and the blessings of God! Leah, like so many women, just longed for love and acceptance only to feel rejected or only good for sex and babies.

Read the scriptural account of the life of Rachel and Leah and reflect on the questions stated.

Continued...

_____

_____

_____

_____

_____

_____

_____

_____

_____

_____

_____

_____

_____

_____

_____

_____

_____

_____

_____

_____

_____

_____

_____

_____

_____

_____

_____

_____

_____

_____

_____

_____

_____

Importantly,

why I shared...

Importantly
why I shared...

I wanted to share because I know I'm not the only woman who has forgiven over and over again (abuse, neglect, and mistreatment), or who has done all they could to make the relationship work but it only continued to cause hurt and disappointment. I also wanted to share how I came to realize how much I contributed to the issues by what I did and didn't do. I know if we can begin to own up to our wrong and really work on us; we can expect our situations to change, also by learning like Hannah and Rachel, to pour our heart out to the only One who can open our womb (so to speak) and change our lives. I know how it feels to keep going back to the relationship over and over again to the point of shame, shrinking back, falling away, settling, compromising, and even giving up on the hope of having a real loving fulfilling marriage because the strongholds are so great. I want to encourage you as I encourage myself that all we need is in God the Father, Son, and Holy Ghost.

In closing, we all know that no one has all the answers. We know that God can do whatever He wants to do; He can bless whom He will. But we also know that God uses people. He calls. He equips. He gives boldness, courage, desire, and ability.

For some we are learning a little more, for some we are being reminded of some things, and for others we are inspired and motivated toward our goals, dreams, and purposes.

In reality, we can't expect men to be all that we're not willing to be. We can't make excuses for our issues and criticize them for theirs. We can't expect the blessings and promises of God, if we don't walk in the ways of God ourselves. Even those who have sought God, served God, trusted God, followed God, and are doing all we can to live for God. We still have to strive to learn, to change, to impart, to show our love and adoration for God, etc. Like Hannah cried out for a son and vowed to give him back to God; let our cry and our commitment go out to God, and like Jacob let us refuse to let go till God blesses us.

I want to encourage you to get what you can from this information. Share what you can with other ladies and ladies in the making. And reach out to other ladies, whether it be to lend a hand or ask for a hand. There is no shame in needing help, and offering help is worth the risk of rejection.

Once again, I was inspired by realizing my own need to be a *lady first* and desiring to develop in the areas that have been so damaging to me and my dreams of fulfillment and marriage. I discovered that I need to first get myself together before expecting a man to be the man I expect him to be. I didn't want to be long and drawn out, but I wanted to share these points to bless others.

Thank you for being a part of *Ladies First*. Please email me your testimonies and feedback to:

writeforyourevent@gmail.com

Titus 2:1-8

But as for you, speak the things which are proper for sound
doctrine: that the older men be sober, reverent, temperate,
sound in faith, in love, in patience; the older women likewise,
that they be reverent in behavior, not slanderers, not given to
much wine, teachers of good things - that they admonish the
young women to love their husbands, to love their children, *to
be* discreet, chaste, homemakers, good, obedient to their own
husbands, that the word of God may not be blasphemed.
Likewise, exhort the young men to be sober-minded, in all
things showing yourself *to be* a pattern of good works; in
doctrine *showing* integrity, reverence, incorruptibility, sound
speech that cannot be condemned, that one who is an opponent
may be ashamed, having nothing evil to say of you.

Inspirational Poems

by Babette Bailey

The Brother Was Right
by Babette Bailey

I was talking to one of my friends at the game the other day;
let me tell yau'll 'bout what was said

Cause I was feeling fed up, my friend thought I was crazy,
she was like girl you done bumped your head

She started talking 'bout this brother she met the other night,
and how he had it going on

I was like whatever child, just give him a little time
and he'll be done moved on

She was like dang why you sound so bitter,
they done messed up your love for the game

I told her girl I'm just tired of these same old players,
they ain't got no new move anyway

She was like hold up you trying to tell me you out the game for
good or just the rest of the season

I told her girl I'm done with these losing teams
and I began to list all my reasons

No commitment, no teamwork, no communication
No honesty, no loyalty, and ol' tired conversation

No sacrifice, no compromise, and always selfish ambition
No affection, no appreciation, too many doggone conditions

Then this brother sitting behind me said he couldn't help
hearing, said he even agreed with me

We looked at each other, then looked back at this brother,
I was like whatever you're selling, I'm not buying

He was like hold up on behalf of the brothers hear me out,
cause there's two sides you know to every story

So, I didn't say nothing else, just folded my arms
and let him speak and what he said really moved me

He said just like you're looking, we're looking too,
and there's some things we're looking for

Like a sense of humor, energy and a good vibe,
and we don't like being ignored

He said we're sensitive too, we've got feelings just like you
and yes we need some attraction

But there's something we need above all those things,
when he said that he really got my attention

He said all these things you want from a man,
can God get the same from you

Are you loyal to God, submitted, committed,
can He trust you and rely on you too

He said the problem is you're not even all those things
you're expecting the man to be

That's why I said you giving up those brothers
for all those reasons you mentioned, I could agree

He said the winning people are on the Lord's side,
He can train you to be an exceptional player

He said you know yau'll be the main ones fouling anyway,
then quick to holla foul on a brother

He said you should try committing yourself to God,
and try giving God all your heart

And you should try marrying yourself to Him,
giving Him your mind, your soul and your body

Let your money be His, your time be His,
let Him teach you how to recognize the counterfeit from what's real

He said unfortunately there are some dogs, some snakes
or whatever yau'll want to call 'em

But there's also some others, some brothers who are ready,
but yau'll not ready for them

He said try giving all that stuff to God,
cause we need yau'll to get yourselves together

And don't be moved unless they say I do,
then you won't feel like another failure

I was speechless the rest of the night;
I know that's hard for yau'll to believe

But the brother was right and I couldn't say nothing else,
all I could do was receive

Love You Anyway
by Babette Bailey

Guess what happened to me,
guess who done showed up

I decided just like they say, I wasn't looking for love anymore,
yau'll I had had enough

This time I was really leaving it all in God's hands,
so I told God to just take the wheel

My prayers had changed from crying and pleading
to surrendering all I could feel

I was thinking I had done that before,
but this time wasn't the same

My whole way of thinking, my heart, my attitude,
everything about me had changed

When I tell yau'll I went from being desperate and broken
From bitter and empty to happiness and hope

To where I could feel love filling me up,
and I could feel my strength renewed

I could feel joy and peace returning to me,
my self-esteem being restored too

Yeah love showed up for me,
but it wasn't like I thought it would be

It felt like something pure and simple,
and it came from inside of me

I wasn't trying or having to perform,
I didn't feel like I had to measure up

I just felt like I had a newfound love for myself,
and that my love for me was more than enough

The love that I was feeling for myself,
it wasn't selfish as it may have seemed

Though I definitely was thinking and intentionally focusing,
and it was at that point all about me

I had given love and tried to love
everything and everybody else

Then I realized I can't love anybody else,
if I fail and neglect to love myself

I started thinking about my happiness,
and thinking about my needs

Thinking about how to take better care of me,
and how I could enhance me

I decided to celebrate myself,
and to speak into my own life

I said first of all I love you girl,
then I said it twice

I told me that you are beautiful,
I told me you're awesome too

I told myself you are valuable,
and I began to do something new

I could see that God had put something
special on the inside of me

He had given me something that made me different,
and creatively unique

My own name, and my own style,
and an irresistible personality

Well maybe not to you, but for that special someone
that will be crazy over me

Till he comes, I'm going to love myself,
and treat me as I expect him to

When he finally shows up and gets to know me,
he'll be thrilled to say I do

So, I thank God for giving me the understanding
and for giving me love for myself

It feels good, it's a little different,
but I know it's going to help

I'll practice till I get it right,
I'll get back up if I fall

And if you see me neglecting myself,
please feel free to give me a call

I want to encourage you God can give you
that kind of love for yourself too

Just ask Him to help you, believe He will,
and watch how God comes through

And if there's something that you don't like
about yourself, strive to find a way

Strive to change it or strive to accept it,
but determine to love you anyway

Yes We Can
by Babette Bailey

I've been standing at the foot of this mountain
trying to figure how in the world I'm gonna get to the other side

I can't see around it, I can't see through it,
and God only knows what it's gonna take to climb

The enemy is talking loud in my left ear,
telling me I can't and I'm foolish to even try to make it

But God's in my right ear saying *Yes You Can,*
tell that mountain to move and go get your promises

I've spoke to the mountain, but it's still in my way,
so intimidating, my God this thing is huge

But I've been stuck at this place so long and I'm sick and tired,
and somehow I've got to make this sucka move

I realize there's no reasoning, this thing ain't got no heart
And I realize in my own strength that I can't get too far

So I'm looking at God and I'm looking at this mountain,
wondering did I hear God clearly is this task for me

But I know it is, cause I can't ignore all these feelings, all these dreams,
these things inside of me just won't leave

So I keep searching for direction,
searching for help

Asking this person and that person,
but I feel like I'm by myself

I know I have faith,
God's done some miraculous things in my life

And I know if God says that I can
that it's only a matter of time

I've just got to do all I can,
I don't want any more time to be wasted

I know that the promises of God are good,
for His goodness I've already tasted

I've felt His wind underneath my wings,
seen Him part the Red Sea for me

As I look back over my life,
I see how He's kept me from things seen and unseen

The fiery darts of doubt,
insecurity and fear

Have threatened me, even pierced me,
but God's been right here

So mountain, get out of my way!
Mountain you've got to move!

God's got a plan destined for my life,
and I've got a job to do

And yes I can make it,
I'm equipped and I'm well able

Yes, I can make it,
because my God is faithful

Our President Barack Obama has told us
over and over again *Yes We Can*

He showed us, God sent him to give us hope
and He's speaking to us through this man

Many are against us,
but there's more on our side

Many are laughing and taunting us,
but God's already decided

God's glory will be revealed,
so let's press our way through

Let's continue to fight the good fight of faith,
cause this mountain has got to move

So when the naysayers and doubters tell us we can't;
we'll tell them, *Yes We Can*

When the doctors give up on us and tell us we can't;
don't fret, just say, *Yes We Can*

When the enemy comes against us to tell us we can't;
declare by the Blood of Jesus, *Yes We Can*

Even when those closest to us tell us we can't;
tell them with all due respect, *Yes We Can*

Additional Works

Additional Works

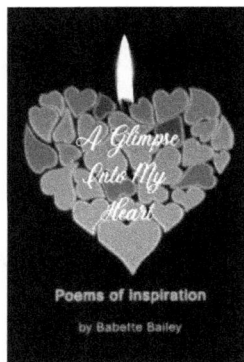

A Glimpse Into My Heart is a collection of poems sparked by many different people, events, hopes, dreams, issues, and a lot of other things that have touched & impacted Babette's heart in different ways.

Just like our lives, like a good song, or like a fresh new idea that could go on and on in our minds, these glimpses are meant to open the heart, gently lift the heart, and bring a spark to the heart that will go on and on.

Babette is glad to have this opportunity to touch your heart by sharing her heart with you. You will not only be able to relate to many of the poems in *A Glimpse Into My Heart*, but you will be inspired, encouraged, lifted up, smile, and even laugh.

A Glimpse Into My Heart is available through major online book retailers, such as, Amazon, Books-A-Million, Barnes & Noble, and Walmart.com. You can also order directly, by contacting Babette Bailey by email: writeforyourevent@gmail.com

Contact Babette Bailey for:
- ❖ *Books of Poetry*
- ❖ *Poetic Calendars*
- ❖ *Greeting Cards*
- ❖ *Home Décor / Canvas Prints*
- ❖ *Ghost Writing*
- ❖ *Spoken Word*
- ❖ *Other Writings*
- ❖ *& Songs of Inspiration*